Frankfurt

An Illustrated Guide
to the Metropolis on the Main

Frankfurt in about 1860, based on a drawing by Scheuren

Text: Wolfgang Kootz
Photography: Willi Sauer and others

Published by Kraichgau Verlag, Germany

The history of the City of Frankfurt

794	Earliest records mention franconofurd, the „Ford of the Franks", as the location of a Frankish Royal Council and a synod of bishops. Its geographically favourable location at the only ford across the Main allows the town to gain rapidly in importance.
11th century	Trade fairs take place for the first time on the Römerberg („Romans' Hill").
1152	The cream of the aristocracy meets in Frankfurt to elect Friedrich Barbarossa to be King of Germany for the first time. Until the „Holy Roman Empire of the German People" comes to an end in 1806, 33 out of a total of 52 kings and emperors are elected here.
1219	The oldest of the present-day churches in Frankfurt, St Leonhard's, is built.
1240	The Emperor Friedrich II grants the city special trade fair privileges, in order that traders who ply their wares here stand under imperial protection on their way to and from the city.
about 1250	Conversion of the Carolinian Salvatorkirche („Church of the Saviour"), built in the 9th century. The early Gothic nave represents the first stage in its development into Frankfurt Cathedral, which was not to be completed until 1877.
1330	The annual Autumn Fair is joined by the Spring Fair.
1349	Persecution of the Jews, following an outbreak of plague.
1356	The city is confirmed in an Imperial Law, the „Golden Bull", as the place at which German kings are to be elected.
1372	Frankfurt becomes a „Free Imperial City", and thus subordinate only to the emperor.
1405	The „Römer" becomes the city's town hall.
15th century	On the Emperor's orders, the city's Jews are banned from the vicinity of the cathedral and confined to a ghetto around the present-day Börneplatz: the „Judengasse".
from 1562	Ten German emperors are crowned in the Imperial Cathedral.
1585	A coin exchange is set up for visitors to the trade fairs, which eventually develops into a major present-day institution, the Frankfurt Stock Exchange.
16th century	The city, which by now boasts 20,000 inhabitants, is one of the most important trading and trade fair centres north of the Alps and has the main trade fair for books in the German language.
1614	Widespread popular fury during a peasants' revolt leads to the plundering of the Jewish ghetto.

17th/18th centuries	The city develops into one of the most important centres of Jewish culture in Germany.
1749	Johann Wolfgang Goethe is born on 28th August in Frankfurt

„Goethe travelling in Campagna" – painting by J.H.W. Tischbein

1816-66	The city is the capital of the „German Federation"
1833	Students storm the „Hauptwache" (the central police station) and release fellow students from the cells.
1848/49	The first freely elected parliament in Germany meets in St Paul's church. The revolution collapses.
1864	The Jewish are given full civil rights.
1866	Frankfurt is annexed to Prussia.
1898	Rows of houses are pulled down to make room for the tram network to be built. The city now has 290,000 inhabitants.
1936	Rhine-Main international airport is opened.
1944	The historic city centre is destroyed in air raids.
1949	The city narrowly fails to be elected the capital of West Germany. It becomes the home of the German Bundesbank (central bank), the Bundesrechnungshof (Federal Court of Audit), and more than 400 commercial banks, making it the financial capital of Germany.
1990	The „Messeturm", the tower on the edge of the „Messegelände" (Exhibition Centre), is completed. With a height of 256 metres (840 ft) it is the tallest office building in Europe.
1993	Frankfurt is chosen to be the seat of the future European Central Bank.

View looking across the Main towards the famous Frankfurt skyline, with modern skyscrapers flanking the towers of the

Dreikönigskirche (Church of the Epiphany) and the Imperial Cathedral.

A city introduces itself

Frankfurt nowadays has about 660,000 inhabitants and no less than half a million jobs, as some 300,000 commuters, visitors, and travellers come into this metropolis on the Main every day. This calls for good traffic access and flexibility, because such enormous numbers of people can only be handled if there is a good local public transport system. The suburban electric and underground railways are the indispensable means of transport for the offices in the city centre, and in the opposite direction for the long-distance trains arriving at "Hauptbahnhof" - the mainline station, which handles one of the largest numbers of passengers of any station in Europe - and at Rhine-Main airport, continental Europe's most important air travel intersection. As the city is also at the point where major European trunk roads intersect, it is the ideal location for the head offices of numerous multinational companies and banks, for international trade fairs and congresses, and for the central organisations of many industrial associations and foreign representations - and also the ideal starting-point for exploring the romantic side of Germany along the Rhine, Mosel, Main, and Neckar.

Nevertheless, this business centre is also well worth visiting in its own right; it has its own unique mixture of historic buildings and skyscrapers in the Manhattan style. There is an unimaginable wealth of traditional and cultural exhibits spread around more than 40 museums, more than 20 theatres present international shows and artists, and numerous libraries and archives serve the citizens, the various colleges and research institutes; so it is no wonder that Frankfurt has one of the largest culture budgets in Germany.

A city of this world standard obviously also offers attractive facilities for shopping. The most popular streets for this are the "Zeil", the shopping street with the highest sales turnover in the whole of Germany, the "Fressgass", and the even more exclusive Goethes-trasse. It is rather more peaceful on the Mainpromenade and in the very generously proportioned belt of parks and gardens around the central area of the city; these are parks and gardens laid out where once the city's defensive walls stood. There are numerous sports grounds lost in the midst of the biggest area of municipal woodland in Germany.

Nearly 2 million visitors, accounting for a good 3 million overnight stays, come to Frankfurt every year, where 19,000 hotel beds in all categories await them. The range of restaurant facilities is just as great, offering a cross-section across every kind of cuisine from all over Europe, Asia, and Latin America, and of course including many that offer traditional German country fare. In the suburb of Sachsenhausen, in particular, there are still local-style pubs and cafés serving "Ebbelwei" (a powerful form of cider), "Handkäs mit Musik" (a cheese speciality), the original Frankfurter sausages, the famous "Grüne Sosse" ("green sauce"), and a cream cake called a "Frankfurter Kranz".

A tour of historic Frankfurt

Am Römerberg

Our route through the historic city centre of Frankfurt starts at its central point, on the **Römerberg ❶**. The oldest historic traces of settlement in Frankfurt are to be found near here, on the hill where the cathedral stands - safely above flood level on the banks of the Main. The Frankfurt "Messen", or trade fairs, once used to be held here on the Römerberg. Merchants used to travel to Frankfurt to the Fair in Frankfurt as long ago as the 11th century, and there has also been a Spring Fair ever since 1330. The Emperor Friedrich II had granted the city a special Trade Fair privilege in 1240 which placed the traders, and their valuable goods, under his protection. At the times when the Fair was being held, the hostels and vaulted cellars with their shops on the ground floor were in short supply all around the Römerberg. In addition to the coarse local cloth they also sold fine lace from France and spices from overseas. Booksellers were also represented at the Fair from an early date onwards. This was the origin of the Frankfurt

The medieval façade of the "Römer", the town hall of Frankfurt. The actual building properly called "zum Römer" can be recognised by the lantern cupola and the balcony bearing various coats-of-arms.

Römerberg: from the "Gerechtigkeitsbrunnen" (Fountain of Justice, 1611), the goddess Justitia reminds the city's representatives to act fairly towards all citizens.

Book Fair, which nowadays has the leading position in the world. Jugglers and conjurors provided entertainment on the thronged streets and squares.

Although the town square on the Römerberg has long since lost its leading position as the trade fair centre to more modern facilities, with gigantic exhibition halls, it still draws millions of visitors during Advent with its traditional Christmas Market. A magnificent Christmas tree, 26 to 30 metres tall, stands out against the romantic background formed by the façades of the Römer or, depending where you are looking from, by the eastern side, with its charming half-timbered gables. Only insiders know that this harmonious-looking row of houses was not built until 1983. Just like their extension, the "Schwarzer Stern" ("Black Star"), these are reconstructions of 15th and 16th century houses which stood here until 1944.

Along the west side, the city had the **Römer** ❷ rebuilt after its destruction in 1944 as correctly and authentically as possible. The side facing the square consists of five medieval façades, behind which is the town hall, itself a symbol of the historic Frankfurt. The name "Römer" comes from the central, and tallest, of the three step-gable structures in which Italian visitors to the trade fair used to be housed. After being rebuilt in the late Gothic style, it served from 1405 onwards together with the building behind it, the "Goldener Schwan", as the town hall. The other four gabled buildings were bought up by the city during the course of the centuries: the renaissance buildings of "Alt Limpurg" (on the left) and "Löwenstein", and other buildings

Renaissance staircase in the inner courtyard of the Römer.

at the back leading right through to the Paulsplatz. It was here in the town hall that the Princes Elector used to negotiate before electing their emperor, and then met for the concluding banquet in the Kaisersaal ("Emperor's Hall") behind the balcony. But the ordinary people had something to enjoy as well; on such grand occasions, the fountains on the Römerberg ran with wine instead of water, oxen were roasted on the spit, and there was every kind of entertainment on hand as well.

At the end of the 19th century, the city had the main elevation of the Römer improved with statues and a balcony on which successful politicians and athletes presented themselves to the cheering public. The Kaisersaal behind it is accessible from the Limpurger Gasse, from which one first comes into a small courtyard, the Römerhöfchen, in which the Hercules fountain (1904) stands. The "Silberberg" house, recognisable by the portal entrance, was built in 1595, whilst the "Goldener Schwan" was first mentioned in historical records in 1322 but did not take on its present form until 1731. The Gothic Schwanenhalle is a reminder of the times when it was built. The Renaissance staircase (1627) and the Limpurgsaal finally bring us in to the highly historical Kaisersaal, which was rebuilt in a simplified form after its destruction in 1944. The collection of more than life-size portraits of 52 German kings and emperors of the Holy Roman Empire of the German nation is still very much worth seeing; they stretch from Charlemagne to Franz II, who abdicated in 1806. The paintings were produced in the years from 1838 to 1852, and emerged unscathed from the air raids of the second world war.

Kaisersaal: portrait of the Emperors Ludwig IV and Karl IV.

Kaisersaal: open daily from 10.00 am to 5.00 pm (except when special events are being held). Tel. 21234814.

Kaisersaal with the portraits of all the German emperors up to 1806.

Alte Nikolaikirche: Memorial plaques to Siegfried zum Paradeis († 1386) and his second wife Katharina zum Wedel († 1378).

11

In the middle of the Römerberg stands the Fountain of Justice (1543) with the goddess Justitia from antique times; she seems to be watching severely, and without the usual blindfold, over the municipal administration centre. Streams of water flow out beneath her from the mouths of animals and from the mouths and breasts of female water-sprites - a customary image in the sensual time of the Renaissance.

The Römerberg is closed to the southern side by the **Alte Nikolaikirche** ❸ (the "old church of St Nicholas"), built in 1290 to replace the old Court Chapel which used to belong to the Saalhof (Court). The high sloping roof was deliberately designed to fit in with the

Historic half-timbered façades on the east side of the Römerberg.

Frankfurt roofscape of those days. From the 15th century onwards it was used exclusively by the city councillors and their families when they attended services. These privileged persons had a magnificent view from the gallery, erected later, down onto great events on the square such as markets, trade fairs, and tournaments. Watchmen posted here not only had to sound horns to warn of the outbreak of fire but also to signal the arrival of ships plying up or down the Main. A carillon of 35 bells is sounded every day at 9.05 am, 12.05 pm, and 5.05 pm from the tower of this old church. On the right of the Alte Nikolaikirche, the Fahrtor street leads down to the Main.

On the right is the Alte Nikolaikirche, once the Councillors' chapel.

The former Saalhof, which now houses the Museum of History. The baroque Bernusbau flanks the medieval Rententurm.

The Romanesque palace, the **Saalhof ❹** used to stand here from the 12th century onwards. Only the palace chapel has been preserved to this day; it is the oldest building in Frankfurt. The present-day complex of buildings also includes the Rententurm (15th century), the corner tower, and the "Palas" of the Stauffer emperors (both of these are reconstructions), as well as the baroque Bernusbau (1715-17), the neo-Romantic Burnitzbau (1842/43), and the modern main building dating from the 1970's - this last set off violent popular protests before it was even finished because it did not fit in architecturally; it hides as if in shame on the rear side, as seen from the Main. This is also the main entrance to the Museum of History, which documents the urban development of Frankfurt from the earliest settlement to the present day. In addition to paintings and portraits of leading personalities, there are also views of the city, drawings, photographs, sculptures, and model buildings, domestic utensils and fashion, the Frankfurt Council Silver and scientific instruments. There are special departments for the Children's Museum and the coin cabinet, and the models of the city are impressive;

Museum of History: *Tu. to Su., 10 am to 5 pm, We. 10 am to 8 pm. Tel.: 212-35599.*
Entrance free on Wednesdays (except to special exhibitions)

Museum of History: the Gontard family's dolls'-house.

Museum of History: coronation insignia of the German emperors (copy made in 19th century)

they show the old centre of Frankfurt before it was destroyed by bombing on 18th and 22nd March 1944, as it was after this destruction, and the situation in the 1980s after its restoration, with the post-modern buildings such as the Schion and those in the Saalgasse. The predominant feature prior to 1944 would have been the half-timbered houses, which were often given preference to brick or stone buildings merely for cost reasons. They all disappeared in the hail of bombs in 1944, which also cost the lives of about 6,000 people.

The rectangular Rententurm, in the street called Fahrtor, nowadays also belongs to the Museum of History. The late gothic Wehrturm (1456) was part of the defences along the Main, and served as quarters for an official called the "Rentenmeister"; his responsibility was to collect the harbour charges. Nowadays, barges are loaded and unloaded in the Osthafen and the Oberhafen before travelling further up the Main. In Fahrtor is also the only half-timbered house to have survived the bombing in 1944 almost unscathed, the Haus Wertheim (about 1600). An artistically designed half-timbered Renaissance structure rises above the ground floor of sandstone arcades.

A pedestrian bridge, the Eiserner Steg, before the impressive silhouette of the Imperial Cathedral.

Close at hand is a pedestrian bridge across the Main, the **Eiserner Steg ❺**. The history of its construction bears witness to the self-assurance of the citizens of Frankfurt, who never had to knuckle the forelock before princes or any other absolute rulers. Because the old bridge, the Alte Brücke, had meant a long detour for many inhabitants, a number of them grouped together and collected the money together to build the Steg. In 1867 the financial arrangements were complete, and work could start; two short years later, the bridge was ready. Anyone who crossed it had to pay a toll of one Kreuzer. This was abolished in 1885 when the city took over responsibility for the bridge.

Back at the Römerberg, we can turn to the prestigious modern buildings filling the square between the Alte Nikolaikirche and the cathedral. Here is the home of the **Kulturzenturm "Schirn" ❻**, the cultural centre of this cultural city. This is where exhibitions are held regularly of the plastic arts and readings held in the Schirncafé. The main entrance facing the market square, a round structure, was inspired by the mausoleum of Theoderich in Ravenna. The name "Schirn" is the word commonly used in the Middle Ages for a group of market stalls, e.g. those of the butchers or the bakers, who plied their wares here in the centre of the city.

The **Struwwelpeter Museum** has been housed here as well since 1994. A collection of books, sketches, letters, photographs, and manuscripts was assembled from the estate of the Frankfurt doctor and world-famous author of children's books, Dr Heinrich Hoffmann (1809-1894), and a number of rare first editions dating from about 1900.

Struwwelpeter Museum: title pages from editions dating from about 1900 in German, English, and Latin (1956)

Struwwelpeter Museum: *Tu. to Su., 11 am to 5 pm, We. 11 am to 8 pm, tel.: 281333. Entrance free.*
Schirn art gallery:
Tu., Fr., Sat., Sun. and public holiday 10.00 am to 7.00 pm, Wed., Thur. 10.00 am to 10.00 pm, tel. 299882-0

In the square in front of the cathedral, the **archaeological Garden** ❼, the city in the 1970's excavated traces of earlier settlement. This hill was high enough to be safe from flood water, and people have been living on it for more than two thousand years. Three lines of walls of different heights show the various epochs in the construction of the various buildings. The low walls are the foundations of two Roman bath houses (75 - 110 AD), the higher ones are part of a Carolinian imperial palace (820 - 850), and the slightly lower ones belong to a late medieval vaulted cellar (14th to 16th centuries) which was much coveted, among other things, as a store for the goods of the merchants.

Archaeological Garden with the foundation walls of a Roman bath house, right, and of a Carolinian imperial palace. In the background is the Schirn cultural centre.

The foundation walls of thesc three epochs are an impressive demonstration of the changes in importance which Frankfurt underwent as it developed from a military to a political to a business centre. The Roman and the Carolinian buildings have also been

View across the excavation site to the west end of the ▶ imperial cathedral with its massive tower.

reproduced as a model, so that visitors can more readily form an impression of these structures.

Only a few metres now separate us from the cathedral, as the parish church of St Bartholomäus has been known since the 18th century. It received the honorary title of **Kaiserdom** ❽, "Imperial Cathedral", because the German kings and emperors were elected here from 1152 onwards, and from 1562 crowned as well. However, it has never been a "cathedral" in the sense of being the See of a bishop.

Work started in 1250, on the site of earlier churches dating from the 7th, 8th, and 9th centuries, on building a three-nave church which is now one of the oldest in the Middle Rhine region. A Gothic Choir and the Reliquary were added in the 14th century. The vaulted roof was completed under the direction of Madern Gerthener, who was also responsible for the infrastructure of the massive west tower. It was not until the church was being thoroughly renovated after the Great Fire of 1867 that the 95-metre high spire was completed.

The south portal under the tower once again shows the skill of Frankfurt people in combining traditional and modern art. Hand-worked copper plates (1958) underneath the lace vaulting of 1422 show pictures from history, with prominent emperors and kings and their connection with the cathedral: at the top is Charlemagne and Ludwig the German, the founder of the original Stiftkirche. In the middle are Otto the Great and Konrad III, and below them Friedrich I, "Friedrich Barbarossa", and Karl IV. The southern portal of the traverse is decorated by seven prophets, bronze reliefs (1962) by Hans Mettel, spanned by an arch bearing numerous figures from the 14th century with a representation of the appearance of Our Lord.

The north portal of the traverse, crowned by its magnificent rose window, is where the kings and their retinue used to leave the cathedral at the end of the coronation ceremony. Whilst the figures on the consoles, the reliefs on either side of the rose window, and the Madonna were already in existence at the time of these processions, the figures in the gable date from the time of the reconstruction, about 1880, and the reliefs of the bronze doors date from 1965 (Hans Mettel). The same artist also created the monumental stone relief a few metres further west, on the closed wall of the crossing.

The neo-Gothic vestry hall leads us into the tower building at the ground floor of the Pfarrturm. Here the original of Backoffen's crucifixion group is on display, the copy of which we have just been able to see outside the cathedral. The organ (1956/57 and 1993/94) in the southern traverse and the Choir is one of the largest in Germany, with 114 registers. The numerous carved Gothic altars were acquired by the city pastor,

Cathedral: *Open to visitors from 9 to 12 noon and from 2.30 to 6.00 pm on working days; only from 2.30 to 6.00 pm on Fr. and Su.; Guided tours at 3.00 pm every day.* **Cathedral museum:** *Tu. to Fr., 10 am to 5 pm; Sa., Su., and public holidays 11 am to 5 pm. Tel.: 289229.*

Mr Münzenberger, after the reconstruction in 1880; he had them restored and in most cases completely reconstructed. They come from various different regions of Germany; the Apostles' Altar (1523) from Saxony, for instance, the Sippenaltar from Ulm, and the Altar of Our Lady (both about 1500) from Bavaria.

Before we reach the Choir, an archway opens to our right revealing the Chapel of the Tomb of Our Lord, which houses an artistically

Kaiserdom: View down the nave into the Choir.

important stone sculpture dating from 1442 representing Our Lord being laid in the Tomb. A door leads from here to the plain and simple chapel in which the German emperors were elected, which from 1438 onwards was at the same time the monastery library. 16 out of 23 German emperors were elected in this room, which today serves as a chapel of worship. Underneath its four cross-vaulted arches, on the newly erected altar, stands a triptych illustrating the Passion (15th century) which originally stood in Unna, in Westphalia. Six small pictures on either side of the cross show scenes from the Passion of Christ and events between His being taken down from the cross to the issuing of the Holy Ghost.

The modern four-piece altar (1993/94) in the centre of the church marks the historic point where the emperors were crowned. Above the choir stalls (1352) runs the restored Bartholomäus frieze (about 1410) which shows the life and martyrdom of the apostle as perceived in

Election Chapel in the Kaiser-dom, now a chapel of worship.

the Middle Ages. It starts on the right of the door to the electors' chapel with the despatch of Bartholomäus on his mission, his success in curing the king's daughter who was possessed by evil spirits, the scene of the baptism of the king and queen, his capture, torture (skinning), and death at the hands of the king's heathen brother, the punishment meted out to the brother, and the king's adoption of the Christian community, in which he took holy orders as a priest.

One particularly magnificent memorial, decorated with coats-of-arms, figures, and ornaments, is dedicated to Count Günther von Schwarzburg. He was elected in Frankfurt in 1349 as a rival king

The modern four-piece altar marks the central point of the Kaiserdom. The vaulted arch to the Choir spans from the northern to the southern crossing.

The imposing memorial, rich in coats-of-arms, for Count Günther von Schwarzburg († 1349).

against Karl IV, but abdicated from this royal office and died in the same year.

The many figures on the High Altar (15th century) once graced the Katharinenkirche in Salzwedel. In addition to the crucifixion it shows the Passion Story of Christ. The only altar to have originated in this cathedral is the Maria Schlaf Altar, to be found in the northern chapel immediately next to the Choir. This work of art was donated in 1434, and shows the death of the Virgin Mary encircled by the 12 mourning apostles, under an artistically ornate panoply, while above them God the Father takes in the soul of the departed.

In addition to a number of other Gothic altars, we can find a number of noteworthy epitaphs and paintings from the 14th century in the northern traverse and a large painting by Van Dyck (1627). Further memorial plaques decorate the northern side-nave, including an impressive piece of baroque work dating from 1691 and plaques dedicated to important local patrician families.

High altar (15th century) in the centre of the Choir, with representations of the Passion story of Christ.

Maria-Schlaf altar (1434), showing the dying Mother of God surrounded by the Apostles.

Leaving the church, we can cast one more glance from the porch to the newly restored crossing, through which the newly elected emperors used to enter the cathedral for their coronations. Nowadays this houses the cathedral museum with its valuable liturgical instruments, Gothic sacerdotal vestments, Baroque ornaments, and jewellery from the tomb of an aristocratic young girl (about 680), and also a reliquary bust of St Bartholomäus.

Bust of St Bartholomäus: Franz Ignaz Berdolt; Augsburg, about 1727, silver.

On a clear day it is well worth climbing to the top of the church tower, although there are more than 300 steps. From here the visitor has a magnificent panorama view across the old city centre of Frankfurt interspersed with skyscrapers and the green belt marking the course of the former city defensive walls.

◀ *View from the tower of the Imperial Cathedral with the Technical Town Hall, the Römer, and St Paul's church, with skyscrapers behind them including the Messeturm, the tallest building in Europe.*

Opposite the tower entrance is the Leinwandhaus ("Linen House"), a large Gothic building dating from 1396 with a gallery and stalls from which linen used to be sold. The building served later as the town jail for a time. The Leinwandhaus, like the cathedral in its present form, was built to plans by the architect Madern Gerthener.

From the 12th century onwards the Jewish community had also lived around the cathedral; the Christian monastery church and the synagogue existed for a long time directly alongside one another. However, expulsion,

The Leinwandhaus (1396) was built at the same time as the cathedral.

persecution, and even pogroms kept on recurring, such as in 1349, when people held their Jewish fellow-citizens responsible for the plague and killed a large number of them. At the beginning of the 15th century the Emperor Friedrich III set about the neighbourhood of the churches and the Jews had to move into a ghetto around the nearby Börneplatz. The street was then called Judengasse ("Jews' Alley"), and these pitiable people lived there from 1462 in an extremely restricted space and surrounded by high walls. In 1614 they once again fell victim to the people's fury, and the ghetto was overrun and plundered. Despite these persecutions, the Jewish community in Frankfurt maintained relatively large numbers, and they were permitted a form of business which

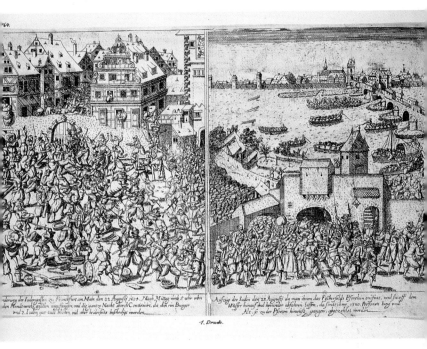

Copper engraving: The Storming of the Judengasse, anonymous.

no Christian was allowed to conduct in those days: interest-bearing loan contracts, with collateral. And in Frankfurt, as has already been mentioned, there was always plenty of trade going on.

In addition to this, Jews were always welcome to the town administration because they were good tax-payers, often lent the city considerable sums, and were even known to write loans off as donations. Frankfurt University, for instance, is to a large extent a foundation endowed by wealthy Jewish residents. One of the most prominent of these was Meyer Amschel Rothschild (1743-1812), the founder of the Rothschild bank in Frankfurt. Only about 100 Jews survived the persecution organised by the Nazis during the Third Reich, which began with a boycott of Jewish businesses in 1933 and escalated into the Reichskristallnacht in 1938, the "night of broken glass", when synagogues were systematically set on fire and destroyed, and culminated in their organised murder in the death-camps. In the **Jewish Museum** in the classical Rothschild palace (1821/22) in Untermainkai 14/15, visitors interested in this period in history are offered an exemplary exhibition showing Jewish life in Germany, and particularly in Frankfurt, from the 12th century to the present day.

Jewish Museum:
Tu. to Su. 10.00 am to 5.00 pm, We. 10.00 to 8.00 pm, telephone 212-35 000. (Entrance free on Saturdays).

From the cathedral we can follow the Kannengiessergasse and then turn left along the Fahrgasse. The Dominikanergasse branches off to the right, and leads past a former nunnery to the city offices on the Börneplatz. The foundations of the houses in the old Judengasse can still be seen in the basement floor, but we will continue on our way along the Fahrgasse to the next cross-roads. The most striking building here is post-modern, in the Pop Art style, the **Museum of Modern Art ❾**. It is shaped like a slice of cake and takes up the whole of the space between three streets.

The striking east façade of the Museum of Modern Art.

Museum of Modern Art: *Tu., Thur., Fr., Sun. 10.00 am to 5.00 pm, We. 10.00 am to 8.00 pm, Sat. 12 to 7 pm, telephone 212-30447, entrance free on Wednesdays.*

The Frankfurt fun-tram: "Ebbelwei express".

Our sightseeing tour now leads us westwards along the Brau-bachstrasse. This was created in 1898, by tearing down a large number of old houses, in order to make space for the modern invention of the day, the "Elektrische" - the tram.

A late medieval house, the Nürnberger Hof, in which merchants from Nuremberg stayed to attend the trade fair, shows how much historical material has fallen victim to progress. It was almost entirely demolished in 1904. A Baroque arched gateway dating from 1720 has been retained in the courtyard at the back of house no. 28; facing it is a late Gothic entrance doorway (15th century) with two arches and a star vault. Braubachstrasse, incidentally, used to be known popularly as the "Red Sea" because most of the houses were built of red brick.

By 1900, Frankfurt's population had increased to 290,000, ne-cessitating an extension of the tram network. It has in the meanwhile greatly lost importance, and has ceded its leading role to the underground railway. The only one that operates from the Römerberg now is Route 11 (Fechenheim) and at the week-end the party-tram, called the "Ebbelwei-Express" [after the local apple-wine brew]. Passengers sit in brightly decorated carriages and enjoy not only Frankfurt's very special drink but also the thronged city centre.

St Paul's church ⑩

Above the Römersberg, the road opens up into the Paulsplatz, where St Paul's church stands, and where a piece of German history was written. This is where the first German National Assembly was inaugurated, on 18th May 1848. While the ordinary people sat and listened from the gallery, the delegates from the numerous German states deliberated on a uniform constitution. The hopes many Germans had harboured of creating one unified state had already evaporated by April 1849, when the Prussian king refused to accept the imperial crown when it was offered to him. Some

St Paul's church was the seat of the preliminary parliament and of the first German National Assembly in 1848/49.

A memorial plaque recalls the political significance of St Paul's Church in the 19th century.

delegates left the Frankfurt parliament in May of that year, and it moved away to Stuttgart.

However, the Assembly had at least drafted a constitution which was accepted by most of the states represented, and so it is justifiable to describe this church as the cradle of German democracy. And even today it stands at the centre of the public gaze just once a year, when the Peace Prize of the German book trade is awarded here.

The building as such pales into insignificance in comparison with its overpowering political significance. Built in the classical style in 1789 - 1833, it was at the time a modern building surrounded by old Gothic architecture. In 1947 it was reconstructed after the wartime destruction, not as a church now but as a national monument. A modern monumental frieze illustrating the 1848 delegates inside the building, and numerous memorial plaques around the outside, recall major politicians and clergymen of the 19th and 20th centuries.

A session in St Paul's church in 1848 - lithography by E.G. May from a drawing by L. V. Elliot

The birthplace of Frankfurt's most famous son, Johann Wolfgang Goethe.

Outside the old city centre

The next building to the left of St Paul's church is the Altes Rathaus ("old town hall"), an extension building put up in about 1905. We pass under a section connecting it with the larger part of the town hall, and then follow the Braubachstrasse, turning right into Kornmarkt and left into Weissadlergasse. At the end, the Grosse Hirschgraben branches off, where deer were kept in the Middle Ages. A few steps further and we reach the **Goethehaus ⓫**, the parental home of the greatest writer in the German language. He was born here on 28th August 1749, and lived here until 1775, when he moved to Weimar. After the war-time destruction in 1944, the city rebuilt the house as an identical copy of the original, so that the visitor here can once again look at a fine example of how wealthy citizens lived in the 18th century.

Goethe's original stand-up desk are to be seen in the so-called Dichterzimmer ("poet's room"), and his puppet theatre in the adjoining room.

Goethe-Haus and Frankfurt Goethe Museum:
1st April to 30th September, Mo. to Sa., 9 am to 6 pm, Su. 10 am to 1 pm; 1st October to 31st March, Mo. to Sa. 9 am to 4 pm, Su. 10 am to 1 pm., tel.: 138800.

Portrait of the poet-prince (by Gerhard von Kügelen).

This is where he wrote his Götz von Berlichingen and Die Leiden des jungen Werthers - the works which were to make him world-famous within a very short time. In the adjoining museum it is possible to follow the "poet-prince's" biography with the aid of pictorial documents, and look at his portraits and those of his contemporaries.

Goethe-Hause: in this room, Goethe wrote the first plays that brought him world fame.

We will now return to the last cross-roads and keep over to the left this time, to reach Rossmarkt and Goetheplatz, turning right to follow Rossmarkt north-eastwards. This very broad street brings us to St Katharine's church and opens up into a square called "An der Hauptwache" - the main police station. The first church in this square is the place where the first Protestant sermon was preached in Frankfurt, in 1522. The Baroque church which later took its place is where Johann Wolfgang Goethe was baptised and later confirmed. The baroque church was rebuilt in 1950, with a simplified interior. Opposite it, and practically on the roof of the underground railway station, is the re-built **Hauptwache** ⑫, dating from 1729. On 3rd April 1833, which was Good Friday that year, students stormed the building shouting the cry of the

Rossmarkt.

The Hauptwache, once a police station and prison, was the focal point of an attempt at a political revolution in 1833.

French Revolution, Liberté, Égalité, Fraternité! and liberated their fellow-students imprisoned here.

Several soldiers were killed in this incident, which was the only attempt at a revolution in Germany during that period. The intended effect, of triggering off further revolutionary uprisings, was not achieved. When the underground local transport station was being built here, the Hauptwache was carried away stone by stone and rebuilt in the identical, authentic form. The location of the former police station and prison is now marked by an unpretentious café.

The Hauptwache and St Katharine's church surrounded by modern office blocks and skyscrapers.

Anyone who by now has had enough of the historic sights of Frankfurt to enjoy can now carry on towards the right and into a street simply called Zeil, the shopping street that generates more turnover than any other in Germany. It is 500 metres long and 34 metres wide, and rows of trees give it a casual feeling. Back in the 14th century it was still outside the Staufermauer, part of the town walls, served as a cattle market, and consisted only of one row of houses - "Zeile" means "row". In those days the shops tended to crowd around the churches, such as the cathedral and St Katherine's. By 1800 Zeil had developed into the most elegant residential street and boulevard in Frankfurt, and more and more shops were established in it. In the building in which Frankfurt's first department store opened in 1907 it is possible today to buy many things, and not only such local specialities as Bembel (a jug of apple wine) and the ingredients for Frankfurt's national dish, Grüne Sosse (which means, literally, "green sauce" - but try it). Any who walks along the milling street with his eyes open will see here, if he has not already noticed it, the multi-cultural variety of the city; indeed, one Frankfurt resident in four is of some other nationality than German.

The shortest route back to the Paulsplatz and the Römerberg is then via Liebfrauenstrasse and Neue Kräme.

Anyone who still feels strong enough to take a further detour can follow the Grosse Eschenheimer Strasse northwards. On the right is the gateway entrance to the former place of the Thurn-und-Taxis princes (1741), standing in front of a first-generation skyscraper, the 79-metre tall Fernmeldehochhaus ("telephone building", 1956). The end of this street is marked by one of the most beautiful Gothic towers in the region, the **Eschenheimer Turm** ⓭ with an attractive version of the Imperial coat-of-arms. As a barbican gate, it formed part of the city's medieval defences from 1428 onwards which have now almost entirely been pulled down to make room for the Anlagenring Platz. (Any street name

The Gothic Eschenheimer Turm used to be a barbican tower forming part of the city's defences in the 15th century.

containing the word "Anlage" is likely to indicate that it is the location of former defences.) Just in front of the tower we can keep well over to the left, go along the Schillerstrasse, and enter the open square in front of the Neue Börse ("new stock exchange", 1879).

The massive statues of animals symbolise the spectacular developments on the securities market, the rising ("bull") market and the falling ("bear") market. The Frankfurt stock exchange, a distant descendant of the coin exchange shop (from 1585 onwards), is now one of the world's major stock exchanges.

As the end of the Börsenplatz we will now follow Börsenstrasse to the left, and at the next cross-roads turn right into the Kalbächer Strasse.

Together with its extension westwards, Grosse Bockenheimer Strasse, it is known popularly simply as "Fressgass" (very crudely translated, "Guzzler's Alley"), because its delicatessen shops, restaurants, and street cafés make it today one of the most popular boulevards in the city. Together with the Goethestrasse, which runs parallel with it to the south, however, it also forms an exclusive shopping zone full of branches of international fashion houses and jewellers.

Neue Börse, Germany's principal market for securities. In the foreground are the symbolic animals of stock markets, the bear and the bull.

The Altes Opernhaus (1880) in the Opernplatz forms a delightful contrast to a modern skyscraper.

The two streets meet together before merging into the **Opernplatz** ⓮, which is dominated by the Altes Opernhaus (1880), dedicated to "True Beautiful Goodness". The panther quadriga recalls another famous opera house, the Semperoper in Dresden. The streams of water from the Marschallbrunnen (1983) contribute to the contemplative flair of the square. Beyond it lies Westend, the district of Frankfurt where the tallest skyscrapers stand. The contrast between historical and modern architecture is particularly striking at Opernplatz, and is quite typical of the metropolis on the Main. A small deviation to the north, along Reuterweg, brings us to Rothschildpark, where a striking sight is Georg Kolbes' "Ring der Statuen" (1954). Our tour, however, takes us along the footpath through the **Taunusanlage** ⓯, starting opposite the façade side of the Altes Oper. Here, and along Gallusanlage that follows it, there is a large number of different memorials. In front of the mirror-faces of Deutsche Bank stands Kolbes' major work, the Beethoven memorial. The same artist created the Heine memorial in 1913. Among the even older memorials are those dedicated to Friedrich Schiller (1864) and Goethe (1844) which portray these poets with laurel wreaths.

At the end of the Gallusanlage, at the other side of Theaterplatz, stands the massive municipal theatre, the Städtische Bühnen, with

A view looking through the mist of the Taunusanlage with the Schiller memorial towards the Deutsche Bank skyscrapers.

The Goethe memorial in the Gallusanlage.

its unusual foyer, 120 metres long and of unusual design. It contains three stages, for opera, drama, and small productions, all under one roof. The city's Education and Culture Department also supports numerous private and independent theatres, acting groups, and cabarets.

Two streets, Weissfrauenstrasse and Münzgasse, lead away to the left, as an extension of Theaterplatz, towards **Karmelitengasse ⑯**, named after the Carmelite monastery that stands there.

The Carmelite monastery: the crossing houses wall paintings by the Swabian painter Jörg Ratgeb (16th century).

The Carmelite monastery: wall paintings by Jörg Ratgeb.

Its church (13th century) was modified in 1424 in the late Gothic style, following plans by Madern Gerthener. In its crossing and in the refectory there are frescoes which the Swabian painter Jörg Ratgeb produced in 1514-23. For his involvement in the Peasants' War, this artist was condemned to death in Pforzheim in 1526 and quartered. The paintings are significant in the history of art, and portray the Passion of Christ and the legend of the Carmelites. The monastery, and an extension building, today house the city's archives and the museum of early and pre-history. Archaeological finds from Roman times onwards, small treasures from classical antiquity, and

Museum of early and pre-history: Pottery ware.

Museum of Early and Pre-history and Archaeological Museum:
Tu. to Su. 10 am to 5 pm, We. 10 am to 8 pm, tel.: 212-35896. Entrance free on Wednesdays.

St Leonhard's church on Mainufer.

St Leonhard's
church:
predella of the
High Altar,
the martyrdom of
St Ursula
(mid-15th century).

St Leonhard's
church:
the "hanging vault".

a collection of finds from western Asia can be seen here. The rebuilt church serves as the main exhibition room.

We can go down Karmelitergasse to reach Untermainkai, which we will follow to the Eiserner Steg. Before reaching it, however, we will pass **St Leonhard's church** ⓱, built in the 13th century. The eight-sided tower and two late-Roman entrances have been preserved from that time; the entrance is now in the interior of the church. The delightful Choir was built in the 15th century, presumably to a design by Gerthener, while the Chapel of the Saviour and the three altars can be attributed to the next later century. The Chapel of the Saviour, a donation from a wealthy family, attracts great attention on account of its "hanging vault". From the Eiserner Steg we can easily return to the Römerberg, thus ending our second circular tour, but from here it is not at all far to the south bank of the Main, Museumufer, and the entertainment district of Sachsenhausen.

Culture and "Gemütlichkeit" in Sachsenhausen

The name of this district, once a separate settlement outside the city, stems according to tradition to the retreat of Karl the Great before the Saxons. The River Main seemed to have cut off the Franconian ruler's route, but a white deer showed him the ford through the river: the "Frankenfurt" - whilst the Saxons "hausten" (camped down) on the south bank.

On the right of the Eiserner Steg is the start of Schaumainkai, also known as **Museumsufer**, as there are no fewer than eight museums along it like pearls along a necklace. They are mainly housed in the huge former mansions which were built by patrician families in the 19th century and are now owned by the city.

The first museum is the **Museum of Arts and Crafts** ⑱, which has been residing in the former Villa Metzler (1802-04) since 1965. This classic-style building was given its massive sloping roof in 1865, and its much admired modern extension in 1985, designed by the New York architect Richard Meier. The museum is divided into a European, an East Asian, and an Islamic department for arts and crafts from the Middle Ages until modern times, and also possesses a significant collection of the book-production and graphic arts from the 14th century onwards. The related **icon museum** (see page 56) has been moved for reasons of space to the nearby Deutschordenshaus, at the southern end of the Alte Brücke.

The next museum westwards is the **Ethnological Museum** ⑲, with exotic statues and cult-house posts in its gardens which invite the visitor to enter and see more. Inside there are collections particularly from Oceania, Indonesia, Africa, and America, arranged according to region and subject.

The first museum west of the Untermainbrücke is the **German Film Museum** ⑳, a permanent exhibition of items from the earliest days of film-making and cinemas which includes films, posters, photographs, equipment, music, and literature. The neighbouring building is the home of the **German Museum of Architecture** ㉑ which presents 20 large models under the heading "From the mud hut to the sky-scraper". It provides an overview of the history of human buildings from the earliest known stone-age huts from near Nice to the metropolis of New York.

Museum of Arts and Crafts: tel. 212-34037
Icon Museum: tel. 212-36261
Ethnological Museum: tel. 212-35391
German Film Museum: tel. 212-38830
German Museum of Architecture: tel. 212-38844
All these museums are open at the following times: Tu. to Su., 10 am to 5 pm, We. 10 am to 8 pm, closed on Mo.

Museums of art and culture along the Main

Top left:
Städelsches Kunst-
institut: Portrait of an
aristocratic lady.

Central picture:
Lichthalle in the Museum of
Architecture

◀ Museum of Arts and
Crafts:
Toiletry table by A. and
D. Roentgen (1769),

Liebieghaus: Athena. ▶

Far right: Post museum.
Wheeled sledge used
by the German
Empire Post Office,
late 19th century.

◀ *Ethnological museum:*
Cow-horn mask

Film museum:
▼ *Ernemann VII A, 1934,*
  Zeiss Ikon AG, Dresden

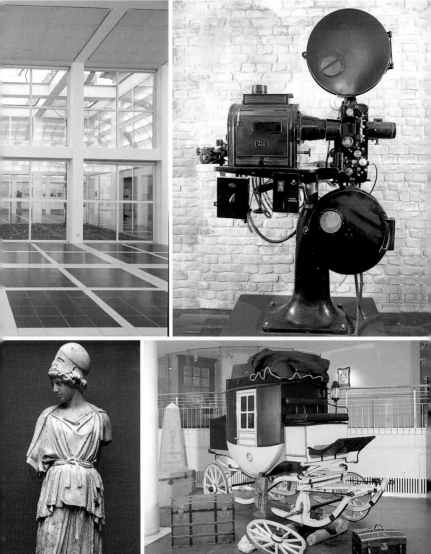

The **German Post Museum** ㉒ is spread out over two buildings at Schaumainkai 53. The visitor can learn about the history of communications with the aid of displays of objects from the early history of the post office and of telephones. An additional source of information is an extensive library, whilst a comprehensive cabinet of stamps awaits the philatelist. Regular visitors will always find new attractions from the constantly changing exhibition areas.

Schaumainkai is always particularly full of people on Saturdays when the gigantic weekly antiques and jumble sale is held. People with modest standards can find something to wear here for small change, and nostalgia freaks can pick up a unique bargain. The point at which Dürerstrasse branches off from Schaumainkai is the start of the big site of the **Städelsches Kunstinstitut** ㉓, an institute of art based on an endowment by a banker, Johann F. Städel. He ordered in 1817 that his collection of almost 500 paintings, together with numerous books and a financial endowment, should form the basis of a foundation which today houses some major works of European painting from the 14th century onwards, as well as sculptures, graphic work, an extensive library of works on this history of art, and a photographic library. 25,000 drawings and 65,000 prints also belong to the collection, making it a real treasure trove for art-lovers.

The next-door building is the **Liebieghaus** ㉔, built in 1896 as the villa of the Baron Heinrich von Liebieg on late Gothic and Renaissance lines. The more recent part of the building, at the back, facing Steinlestrasse, fits in harmoniously with Baroque and Rococo styles. Columns and sculptures enliven the gardens with their imposing old trees and indicate the villa's role as a "museum of ancient sculpture". The Baron made over his property for a nominal price to the city of Frankfurt in 1904 on condition that it should be used "for all eternity" as an art museum, and since then sculptures from Egyptian, Greek, and Roman antiquity have rubbed shoulders with east Asian art and works from the Middle Ages, the Renaissance, and the Baroque period. Contrary to the original concept, the collection has been augmented with individual pieces from the classical period.

The best-known of these individual pieces are the Roman copy of the goddess Athena (the Greek original, from the sculptor Myron about 470 BC, has vanished), a medieval altar relief (by della Robia, about

German Post Museum: *tel. 60600*
Städelsches Kunstinstitut and Municipal Gallery:
tel. 6050980
Liebieghaus-Museum for old sculpture: *tel. 212-38617*
All these museums are open at the following times:
Tu. to Su., 10 am to 5 pm, We. 10 am to 8 pm, closed
on Mo.. Entrance free on Wednesdays.

Liebieghaus: the villa of Baron Heinrich von Liebieg on Sachsen-hausenufer, built in about 1900 in a historical style, and now a museum.

53

1500), and a bronze statue of the Apollo Belvedere (16th century). If we leave the Eiserner Steg to our left, the embankment road will lead us in the direction of the entertainment district of **Alt-Sachsenhausen** ㉕. We first pass the neo-Gothic Church of the Epiphany, which has stood since 1880 on the site of the Spitalkapelle ("hospice chapel", 13th century). At the southern end of the Alte Brücke stands the spreading bulk of the former Deutschordenshaus, a Baroque building in three wings built in 1709 - 15 on the foundations of an earlier Gothic building.

Kuno von Münzenberg had endowed a hospice here in the 12th century, which was then taken over by the Deutsche Orden, a chivalrous order of knighthood, in 1207. The Order's catholic church of St Mary was built in the Gothic style and dedicated in 1309.

Sachsen-hausen: the church of the Epiphany

***Snap-shots
of
enjoyable
moments
in Alt-
Sachsenhausen***

The Gothic façade was added in 1747 - 51 so that the building would match the Deutschordenshaus. Today the complex of buildings serves various purposes, but it is still mainly devoted to the Deutsches Orden. Part of it houses the extensive collection of icons belonging to the Museum of Arts and Crafts.

Grosse Rittergasse branches off from Sachsenhäuser Ufer and leads directly into the heart of Frankfurt's Ebbelwei district. This is where the groups of people lived who were the first to gain a little privilege: small craftsmen, fishermen, gardeners, and women who kept market stalls. Just as vintners sell the wine they have produced themselves all around the Drosselgasse in Rüdesheim, so the Sachsenhausen gardeners offered their home-made drink, an apple wine comparable with farmhouse cider, in Strausswirtschaften or "hedgerow pubs". This has developed over the years into a tourists' amusement district in which more than 200 pubs and taverns jostle for custom from international visitors from late afternoon onwards. Simple tables and benches stand on the cobbled streets in sunny weather and provide a vast amount of seating capacity between the romantic half-timbered houses and just as much German *Gemütlichkeit* - warm, cosy, friendly, easy-going relaxation - in the midst of historical buildings. The street names exude pure historical romanticism: Grosse Rittergasse ("large knights' alley"), Kleine Rittergasse ("small knights' alley"), Paradiesgasse ("paradise alley"), Abtsgäschen ("abbot's lane"), and Klappergasse ("clatter" or "chatter alley").

Two former customs and sentry posts in the classical style dating from 1810 have been preserved in Affentorplatz. The name of the square, which means "monkeys' gate" square, comes from the *Aue*, or water-meadows, to which the gate once led. In old handwriting, however, the 'u' was often written like a 'v', was later read as such, and later still was turned into 'ff'; and Affe is 'monkey'. Even better

Alt-Sachsenhausen:
Kuhhirtenturm, the only survivor of five watch-towers.

known, and celebrated in a rollicking song in years gone by, is a fountain called the Frau Rauscher Brunnen in Klappergasse. The figure on it, which represents a market-stall woman, sprays jets of water at irregular and unexpected intervals over the street and any visitors within range, which is always good for a laugh.

Of the five watch-towers which used to guard this part of the city, on the Kuhhirtenturm ("cow-herds' tower") remains; it also used to be known as the "Elephant", on account of its girth. The composer Paul Hindemith lived in this four-storey tower from 1923 to 1927; he was assistant conductor at the opera house at the time. The only way of bringing his concert grand piano into the building was to remove the roof and lower it in with a crane.

Outside the central area

A place to park the car is just as much of a rarity in Frankfurt as in all the major German cities, so the best way to visit the sights described in the following section is by tram or by bus. For this purpose it is best to buy a whole-day, weekly season, or hotel guest's ticket; these are available at hospitable prices and permit the holder to travel on public transport without limit.

Thus the **Zoological Garden** to the east of the central area can best be reached by underground (Station Zoo). It was founded in 1858, and although it suffered destruction in the second world war it later blossomed rapidly under its director Bernhard Grzimek to become the zoo with the greatest number of visitors in Europe. More than 5,000 birds, animals, reptiles, and insects representing almost 600 species enliven the modern cages and pens - but the visitor is not separated from the creatures by bars. There is even a "free flight" building in which birds and humans are not separated from one another at all. One particularly fine sight is the Exotarium, an artificial landscape with interesting animals all in their natural climatic conditions. Another is the nocturnal animals' house, in

which day and night are reversed so that the animals can be seen behaving in their natural, lively, and attractive way.

To the north-east of the city centre is **Bornheim,** once a separate village but incorporated into Frankfurt as long ago as 1877. Today it is the suburb with the largest number of inhabitants. Berger Strasse runs through the middle of it; this is one of the longest streets in the whole city, and at the same time a shopping street. On Wednesdays and Saturdays a market is held around the Uhrtürmchen, the clock tower, which draws large numbers of visitors. The further we travel from the city centre the more village-like this street becomes, narrower and twistier, lined by inviting guest-

The clock tower in the market square of Bornheim.

houses and wine bars. Here, in the heart of the old "Bernem", one of the most pleasing sights is the half-timbered Altes Rathaus, richly decorated in authentic Baroque shapes.

The extension of Berger Strasse leads to the suburb of Bergen-Enkheim, which has a medieval town centre around its old town hall; we can reach it easily by bus. Apple-wine parlours steeped in tradition invite the passer-by to come in and rest a while. From up here we have a panorama view across to Frankfurt and its imposing skyline, and it is here at the beginning of September each year that the famous "Berger Markt" *Volksfest* takes place, in conjunction with Frankfurt's oldest cattle and pig market. Underground railway routes 6 and 7 lead westwards to the underground

The highly original underground station entrance at Bockenheimer Warte, with the Messeturm in the background.

Bockenheimer Warte, a historic watch-tower in the northern part of this district of Frankfurt.

station at **Bockenheimer Warte**. The highly original entrance to it looks like an underground railway wagon taking a steep bend.

At the northern end of the Zeppelinallee is one of the finest former defensive towers to have been preserved, the Bockenheimer Warte. On the south side of the underground railway we come to the main entrance of the **Senckenbergmuseum** of natural history, in the Senckenberganlage. This goes back to an idea proposed by Goethe, and an endowment from one Dr Senckenberg, which led to the foundation of a scientific research society (1817) and to a famous collection (from 1822 onwards). The present museum and research institute were built in 1907. There is an impressive variety of prints and bones from extinct animals on the ground floor, including the skeletons of dinosaurs up to 20 metres long. The upper floors are devoted to the animal kingdom of today. A total of more than 400,000 exhibits offer the visitor a glimpse of the incredible variety of Nature.

Passing the neighbouring buildings of the university, we can return

Senckenberg Natural History Museum:
Mo., Tu., Th., and Fr., 9 am to 5 pm; We. 9 am to 8 pm; Sa., Su., and public holidays 9 am to 6 pm; tel.: 75420.

▲ *Dwarf elephants from Sicily, Ice Age*
◀ *Snake-necked dinosaur, Jurassic Age*
▼ *Tyrannosaurus, Cretaceous Age*

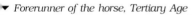
▼ *Forerunner of the horse, Tertiary Age*

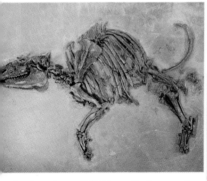

▼ *Beaked dragon, Cretaceous Age*

▼ *Three-horned dinosaur, Cretaceous Age*

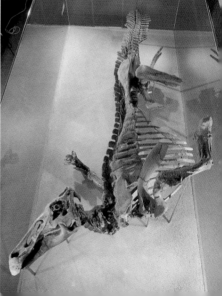

to the cross-roads with the underground railway station. We turn right into Bockenheimer Landstrasse and then left into Palmengartenstrasse, from which we can enter the Frankfurt citizen's favourite park, the **Palmengarten.** It was created by local citizens in 1868 to serve both scientific and recreational purposes. The palm house, built in 1869, is one of the largest glass houses in the world, and contains sub-tropical plants, whilst the Tropicarium provides a glimpse of the plant world in desert, semi-desert, and wet tropical regions. Other glass houses accommodate insect-catching plants and bromeliads, and the latest decorative plants are to be seen in the Blütenhaus ("blossom house"). The gardens are arranged by subject-matter, and display luxuriant blossoms all year round. By way of entertainment there are playgrounds for children, boat and train rides, and mini-golf course. Along the north-eastern edge are the botanical gardens and the Grüneburg park. The banker mentioned before, Meyer Amschel Rothschild, had an English garden landscape laid out here at the beginning of the 19th century, and with its present 29 hectares (over 70 acres) is one of the largest municipal parks anywhere.

The massive Europaturm can be seen from the far side of the Miquelallee motorway access point, and in the other direction are the modern skyscrapers of the Westend district.

From the southern exit from the Palmengarten it is not far to the

A view across the summer flower-beds in the Palmengarten towards the glass houses of the Tropicarium, with the Europaturm.

Heinrich Hoffmann Museum, which like the Struwwelpeter Museum mentioned above is dedicated to the creator of this world-famous figure. Heinrich Hoffmann was a consultant doctor at the municipal mental hospital, and became famous as an author of children's books which he illustrated himself. Bus route 36 links the eastern exit of the Palmengarten with Holzhausenstrasse, which borders the **Adolf von Holzhausen Park.** This once belonged to one of the most respected Frankfurt patrician families, which had a Baroque-style moated grange built here in the style of a country mansion. Today it is owned by the city and serves as a home for the Frankfurter Bürgerstiftung, a citizens' foundation.

The city has placed its modern exhibition centre, the **Messegelände,** along the north side of the main rail freight station. In addition to numerous exhibition halls there are also congress auditoria and ball-rooms integrated into the complex of buildings which have become well known in Germany through such events as major sports fixtures

Frankfurt's modern exhibition centre with its symbol, the 256-metre tall Messeturm.

Exhibition hall in the Frankfurt Messegelände.

like the annual indoor athletics tournament and the six-day cycle races. Amongst the most important of the 25 to 30 major exhibitions which take place here every year are the Spring and Autumn Trade Fairs, which continue a long tradition, as well as the Book Fair and the International Motor Show. Until a few years ago the modern gate house, the symbolic entrance gate to the city, was regarded as the trade-mark of the Messegelände, but its place has now been taken by the **Messeturm.** It is the tallest office building in Europe, with a height of 256 metres. Nearly 3,000 people work in it. For security reason, it is only these employees who are allowed to enter it. In front of its pink granite and glass outside walls stands the 20-metre tall black sculpture of the "Hammering Man".

The journey by suburban electric railway from the main railway station Hauptbahnhof to the western suburb of **Höchst** takes about 20 minutes; it is best known today as the home of the giant chemical company, Hoechst AG. To celebrate its 100th jubilee in 1963, the company built an enormous hall with a capacity of 4,000 people, the Jahrhunderthalle ("century hall"). However, there are also venerable old half-timbered houses, sturdy defensive walls, and the Altes Schloss dating from the times when the town belonged to the Prince Electors of Mainz, and many of these buildings are in a fine state of preservation. The Carolinian Justinuskirche, consecrated in 850 AD, can also be visited on request, as can the museum in the Altes Schloss. A guided tour of the traditional porcelain factory can also be arranged on request.

▲ *Historic town centre*

Schlossplatz ▼

▲ *Schloss in Höchst*

Bolongaro palace ▶

▼ *Beautifully preserved half-tim-*
bered façades

Just before the start: the cycle race "round the Henninger Turm".

The **Henninger Turm,** in the Sachsenhausen district, has made a name for itself mainly because of the cycle race which is held regularly round this tower. From the rotating restaurant at the top, 101 metres above the ground, the visitor can enjoy a wonderful panorama view. To its south stretches a huge area of forest, the **Stadtwald;** with 4,300 hectares (over 10,000 acres, and over 16 square miles) it is the largest stretch of woodland owned by a local authority anywhere in Germany and the favourite hiking area for the citizens of this metropolis. Its special attractions include the woodland educational path, with a fine stand of ancient timber, the Goetheturm providing a magnificent view across the city to the foothills of the Taunus in fine weather, and the numerous weirs and ponds all over the recreational park. An artificial mountain, called "Monte Scherbelino" ("Scherben" are smashed fragments), was created from the rubble of the second world war.

Numerous sports facilities have established themselves further to the west: a horse-racing course, a golf course, the buildings of the Hessen and German Sports Federation, the German School of Gymnastics, and the German Football Federation, not forgetting the **Waldstadion** which is the home ground of Eintracht Frankfurt, a first division football club and the venue for many major sporting events. This stadium is readily accessible from the nearby motorway cross-roads, the "Frankfurter Kreuz", and from Frankfurt **airport.** For a small fee, the visitor can go onto the huge viewing terrace and have a fine view of the lively air traffic, and can also use the visitors' railway. The entrance fee also includes a visit to see some interesting vintage aircraft. Nowadays the airport handles about 31 million passengers and 340,000 aircraft movements a year, or an average of 93 flights a day, making it the busiest air travel cross-roads on the continent of Europe.

Festivals and markets

The feeling which the population has of all belonging together is reflected in more than 100 festivals and markets during the course of the year, almost half of them being organised by the city's tourist office. Those which originated in medieval custom include, for instance, Wäldschestag, Dippemarkt, and the Mainfest - the latter can be traced all the way back to 1393. On Wäldschestag, officially known as "Frankfurt's National Holiday", it used to be customary for the guilds to travel out to the Stadtwald for a picnic on the Tuesday after Whitsun, and Dippemessen were market days when pots and stoneware were sold. Just as with the Mainfest, which used feature contests for catching live fish with a knife, plucking a goose, and performances of Passion plays, visitors can enjoy modern popular entertainment as well as historical contests and presentations. A more recent major arrival is the weekly jumble sale, whilst the romantic Christmas market can look back on centuries of tradition. It attracts some three million visitors every year, making it one of the biggest in Germany. The magnificent gable façades and St Nicholas' church in the Römer form its backdrop every year, as does the 26 to 30 metre tall Christmas tree.

A moving sight: the Christmas market in front of the magnificent backdrop of the Römer.

Tips and addresses from A to Z (telephone area code 069)

Airport: information tel: 690-30511, visitors' terrace tel. 690-70069

Ambulance: tel. 490001

Arrangement:
info, tel. 212-38990

Bicycles for hire:
Theo Intra, tel. 342780

Boats for hire:
Heinz Berghof, tel: 06421/78463;
Otto & Vera Dreyer, tel. 621935

Bowling: Bowling- and Kegelzentrum Rebstock, tel. 702070;
Brunswick Bowling Anlage, tel. 681700

Cinemas:
telephone information 11513/11514

Emergency dispensing chemist:
tel. 11500

Emergency dentist: tel. 6607271

Emergency doctor: tel. 19292

Fitness centres: Fitness Gallery, tel. 294528; Sportfabrik der FTG-Frankfurt, tel. 9707210

Handicapped persons: City guide for the handicapped, tel. 212-35771.
Travel requests: tel. 748090 or 547015

Information:
Tourismus+Congress GmbH Frankfurt am Main, Kaiserstr. 56, tel. 212-38800. Information at Railway station: opposite Plattform 23, Monday to Friday 8 am to 9 pm, Saturday, Sunday + Public holiday 9 am to 6 pm. Information at Römer: Römerberg 27, daily 9 am to 6 pm.

Fire brigade (emergency number):
tel. 112

Golf:
Frankfurter Golf-Club eV, tel. 6662318; Idstein-Wörsdorf Golf-Club, tel. 06126/9322-0;
Neuhof Golf Club, tel. 06102/327012

Horse-riding: Frankfurter Reit- und Fahrclub eV, tel. 6667585;
Reiterbund Frankfurt eV, tel. 6667485

Lost-property office: Mainzer Landstr. 323, tel. 75002403; Airport, tel. 69066359; public transport 213-22258

Messe (trade fairs and exhibitions):
tel. 7575-0

Museums:
see information in this book

Palmengarten: tel. 212-33939

Police (emergency number): tel. 110

Post offices: Main post office, Zeil 110, tel. 909010, Monday to Friday 9 am to 6 pm, Saturday 9 am to 1 pm. Railway station office, tel. 24242712, Monday to Friday 6.30 am to 9 pm, Saturday 8 am to 6 pm, Sunday 11 am to 6 pm

Railway information (Bundesbahn):
Railway station information, tel. 19419, Airport information, tel. 691844

River trips: KD steamship line agency Malachi Faughnan, tel. 285728; KD agent Peter Kleibert, tel. 06131/613642; Primus Line Anton Nauheimer GmbH, tel. 281884; Wikinger Line A.-U. Nauheimer, tel. 282886, 293960.

Room reservations:
tel. 212-30808

Sight-seeing tours: daily bus tours start at Römer and Railway station, also possible individual and special tours and arrangement, tel. 212-38953

Swimming baths:
Brentanobad, tel. 212-39020/19;
Bornheimer Hang, tel: 462340;
Titus Thermen, tel. 95805-0

Tennis:
Tennis & Squash Park Europa, tel. 532040;
Füssenich tennis centre tel. 542318

Theatre, opera, ballet:
Schauspiel, tel. 21237999; Ballett, tel. 21202; Oper, tel. 21237333; Alte Oper, tel. 1340-400; Die Schmiere, tel. 281066; Tiger Palast, tel. 9200220

Zoological garden: tel. 212-33715

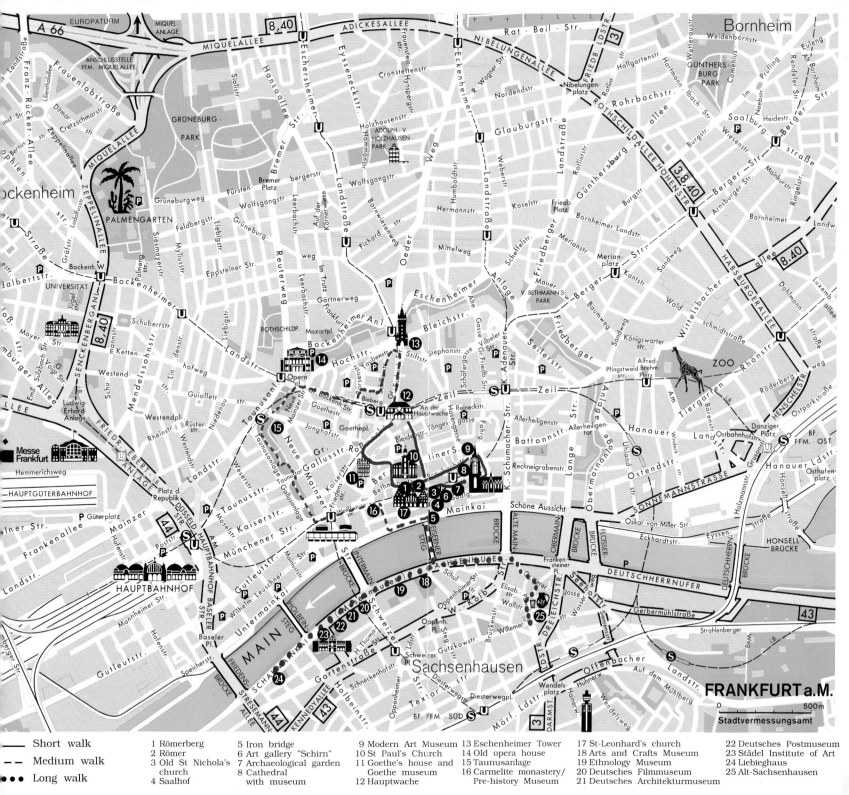

FRANKFURT a.M.

0 _____ 500m

Stadtvermessungsamt

— Short walk
- - Medium walk
••• Long walk

1 Römerberg
2 Römer
3 Old St Nichola's church
4 Saalhof
5 Iron bridge
6 Art gallery "Schirn"
7 Archaeological garden
8 Cathedral with museum
9 Modern Art Museum
10 St Paul's Church
11 Goethe's house and Goethe museum
12 Hauptwache
13 Eschenheimer Tower
14 Old opera house
15 Taunusanlage
16 Carmelite monastery/ Pre-history Museum
17 St-Leonard's church
18 Arts and Crafts Museum
19 Ethnology Museum
20 Deutsches Filmmuseum
21 Deutsches Architekturmuseum
22 Deutsches Postmuseum
23 Städel Institute of Art
24 Liebieghaus
25 Alt-Sachsenhausen

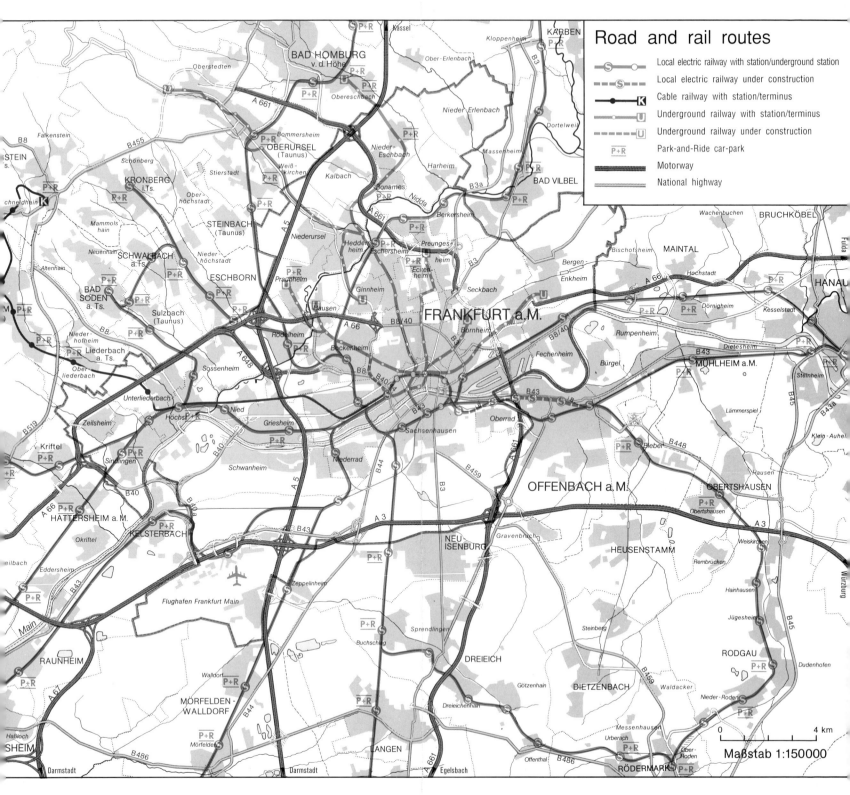

Road and rail routes

Ⓢ—○	Local electric railway with station/underground station
Ⓢ- - -	Local electric railway under construction
●—Ⓚ	Cable railway with station/terminus
○—Ⓤ	Underground railway with station/terminus
Ⓤ- - -	Underground railway under construction
P+R	Park-and-Ride car-park
▬▬▬	Motorway
▬▬▬	National highway

Maßstab 1:150000

0   4 km